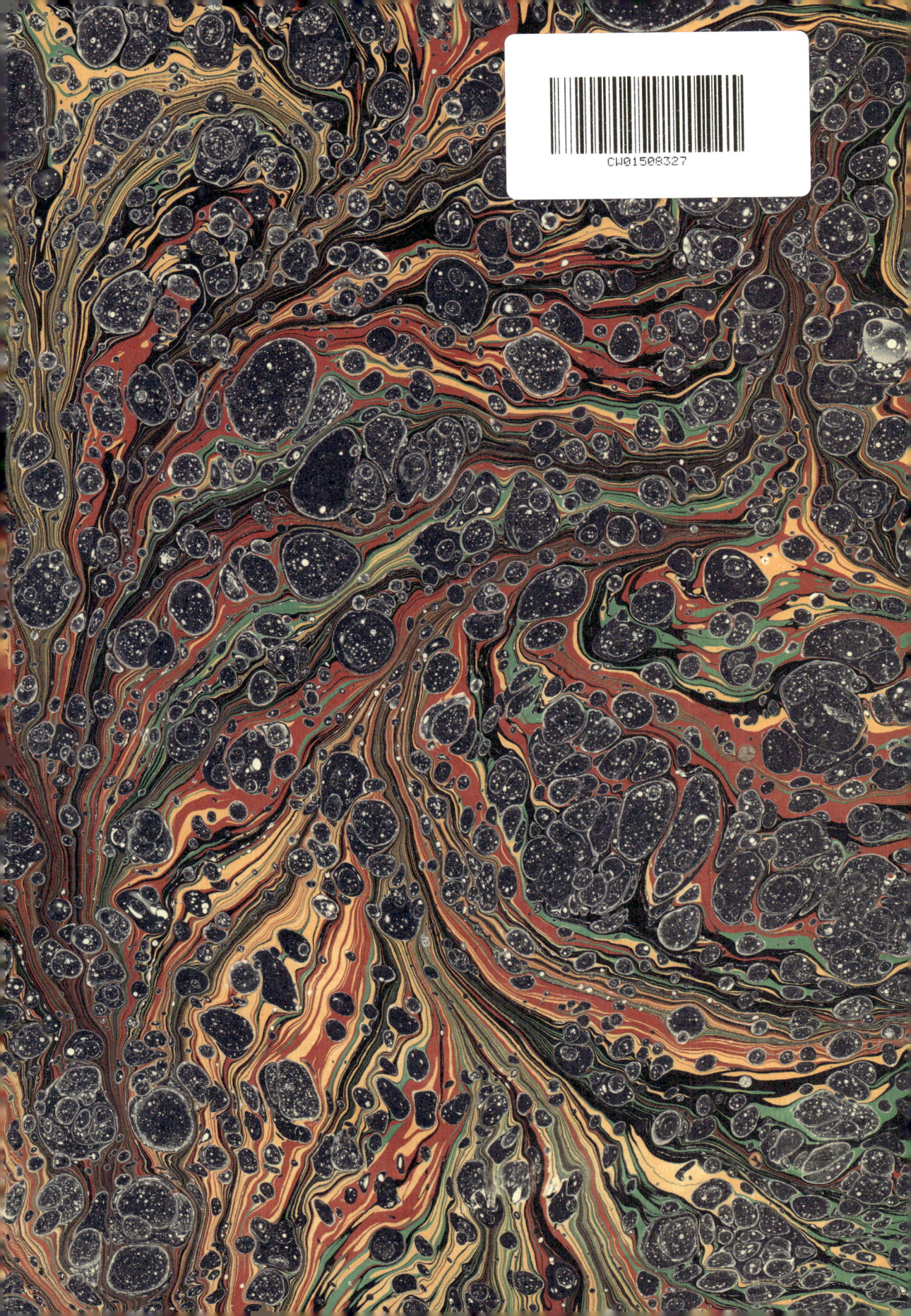

CW01508327

THE GERMAN SNIPER BADGE

1944-1945

Rolf Michaelis

Schiffer Military History
Atglen, PA

Book Translation by Dr. Edward Force.

Book Design by Stephanie Daugherty.

Printed in China.
ISBN: 978-0-7643-4032-1
This book was originally published in German under the title
Das Scharfschützen-Abzeichen, 1944/1945.

We are interested in hearing from authors with book ideas on related topics.

Published by Schiffer Publishing Ltd.
4880 Lower Valley Road
Atglen, PA 19310
Phone: (610) 593-1777
FAX: (610) 593-2002
E-mail: Info@schifferbooks.com.
Visit our web site at: www.schifferbooks.com
Please write for a free catalog.
This book may be purchased from the publisher.
Try your bookstore first.

In Europe, Schiffer books are distributed by:
Bushwood Books
6 Marksbury Avenue
Kew Gardens
Surrey TW9 4JF, England
Phone: 44 (0) 20 8392-8585
FAX: 44 (0) 20 8392-9876
E-mail: Info@bushwoodbooks.co.uk
Visit our website at: www.bushwoodbooks.co.uk

Contents

Foreword

A lack of raw materials near the end of World War II resulted in the Wehrmacht being very limited in its capability. They had neither enough aviation gasoline for the Luftwaffe nor sufficient reserves of fuel for the armored and motorized ground troops. While the focus had previously been on technical superiority, now these reasons put the main burden of the combat back on the simple rifleman.

Thus the strategic importance of single combat was stressed in highly stylized propaganda. No matter if it concerned men who tried to use antitank weapons to take over the tasks of their own tank and tank-destroyer units, which were of only limited use, or the sharpshooters who were supposed to decimate the enemy and save ammunition.

For the latter, Hitler created the Sniper Badge on August 20, 1944. It was to impel soldiers to train and be used as snipers. Since the soldiers themselves to a very special extent were in sight of the enemy troops, and beyond that, unlike the members of other service arms, experienced the death of their enemies directly, the numbers of volunteers did not reach the planned extent.

In this book, this badge, as well as the actions of snipers in general, shall be examined. It is thus an addition to already available literature. But it cannot show the suffering that the war caused humanity. The reader should keep this in mind.
I thank all those who helped in its publication, particularly Mr. Timo Schicke, and Mr. Tammiksaar, who made the materials of his museum available.

Rolf Michaelis
Berlin, December 2010

Two German snipers in World War I. While the seated soldier has mounted the telescopic sight, the standing man still carries his in its shoulder-strap container.

Outline of Sniper History

When one speaks of snipers today, one thinks at once of soldiers equipped with outstanding optics (telescopic sights) and precision weapons. Actually, though, there were selected and encouraged marksmen already in the days of muzzle-loaders. A prominent victim of them was, for example, the British Admiral Nelson, who was killed by a French sharpshooter in the battle of Trafalgar on October 21, 1805. The shooter climbed the mizzenmast of the French ship of the line Redoubtable and, despite the current, was able to get off a well-aimed shot at the commander of the British Mediterranean Fleet.

Even to World War I, the military declined on principle to use telescopic sights, although numerous optics for civilian hunting weapons had been produced since the latter half of the 19th century. Many of these telescopic sights used by German hunters were finally brought in by the military during the course of World War I. There the use of snipers equipped with them in battles of machinery and wear, their tasks including unnerving and psychologically depressing the enemy soldiers in the opposing trenches, even in lulls in the battle. Thus in practice they were constantly kept at their narrow dugouts, which often resulted in nervous breakdowns (so-called "bunker choler"). Erich Maria Remarque also had the protagonist of his novel *All Quiet on the Western Front* be killed by an enemy sniper when he needlessly leaned over the rim of his trench to touch a butterfly.

The names of the so-called machine-gun sniper units formed in the German Army as of the autumn of 1916 were somewhat misleading. They neither would nor could be used as snipers, but were supposed to have a certain special military spirit anyway. The high command at first reserved the use of these units for itself. In fact, the machine-gun sniper units differed more in strength than in usefulness from the hitherto existing machine-gun or mountain machine-gun units. The latter were usually of only company strength, while the machine-gun sniper units had three companies.

Although there was already specific training with telescopic-sight rifles, the German snipers in World War I remained a numerically insignificant weapon group. In the Weimar Republic too, the army command did not give the training of snipers any great importance. Thus the units had rifles with telescopic sights, but they received no thoroughgoing training. Nevertheless, as ordered on January 27, 1928, shooting medals for non-commissioned officers and men were introduced.[1] They consisted of a chevron opening upward, with 8 cm arms, made of an aluminum-colored braid 8 mm wide. A middle stripe 1.5 mm wide was worked

---

1 Heeresverordnungsblatt 1928, No.56, of January 27, 1928.

Inducted at age 17, Musketeer Einenkel had to be trained on a telescopic-sight rifle, and at age 18 he was already promoted to NCO for bravery in the face of the enemy.

into it.[2] The emblem was worn under the braid, 8 cm long, for good shooting achievement. It consisted of stripes of various width – depending on the level – worn on the left forearm.

Though the National Socialists also gave a high value to the military training of racial comrades, the importance of sharpshooting was meager for a long time. The marksman's cord introduced in 1936[3] to replace the Reichswehr's earlier shooting emblems no longer included a special emblem for sharpshooting, as the earlier ones had. The statement in the Army Service Regulation 102 of May 26, 1937, under:

> "C. Performance of the Troops in positions:
> Every opportunity to cause harm to the enemy is to be utilized. The location of snipers to fire on individually appearing enemy targets by day is thus of special value and therefore necessary."

Referred, of course, to the action, but not to any special strategic significance of sharpshooters. In the spring of 1941, in fact, the awarding of marksmen's cords was halted.[4] In general, the modern armored troops and the Luftwaffe were seen as having a much more decisive role, which came to apply to the Allies as well in the end.

But different values prevailed in the Waffen-SS. As in many areas (such as camouflage clothing), it went its own way as to the strategic value of snipers, and in 1940 it was already planning the establishment of separate sniping companies. At this time one will not consider it possible, but poachers confined to prisons and jails were to be recruited for these units! The Reichsführer-SS wrote to the Reich Justice Minister, Dr. Guertner, on March 29, 1940:

> "The Führer has ordered that all game hunters, especially those from Bavaria and Austria, who have broken the law not with nooses, but by hunting with guns, be freed from the serving of their sentences for the duration of the war through service in the special sniper companies included in the SS, and can earn amnesty through good behavior."

The intended establishment of these companies did not take place. Instead, the unit first named the "Oranienburg Poacher Command" in June 1940 was renamed the "Dirlewanger Special Command" in June 1940 and sent to the General Government for security and guard tasks.[5] Although the formation that served in the General Commissariat of White Ruthenia since 1942 fought almost exclusively against partisans, it had rifles with telescopic sights and requested 120 more such

---

2   This badge could be awarded, according to Army Instruction Sheet 1936 No.918 of September 14, 1936, until the summer of 1936, and was then discontinued and not replaced.
3   Army Instruction Sheet 1936, No.652, of June 29, 1936.
4   Army Instruction Sheet 1941, Part B, No.100, of February 14, 1941.
5   See also Michaelis, Rolf: The SS "Dirlewanger" Special Command, Berlin 1998.

This Reichswehr NCO
Wears the chevron-
shaped sniper badge
under the shooting medal
introduced in 1928
(4th class, with four
thin braids).

In 1936 the shooting
braid, some 23 cm long,
braided of aluminum
threads, was introduced.
The NCO here wears the
1st class.

telescopic-sight rifles from Berlin in June 1943. These weapons were used in action against partisans in the countless White Russian wood and swamp areas.

After the Russian campaign began, the Red Army confronted the German troops and their allies with snipers of completely unknown numbers and quality. The USSR was a large-scale pioneer not only with paratroops and armored troops, but also snipers. Practically compelled to react, the Wehrmacht and Waffen-SS now began to push the training and use of snipers. This went so far that even in the pre-military Hitler Youth training, especially talented boys were given specific shooting instruction, for which they could receive the "HJ Shooting Medal for Sharpshooting."

While the snipers were used at first mainly to knock out "selected" enemy officers, NCOs or specialists, in the course of resource shortages it followed that they were used very pragmatically to decrease enemy manpower strength. The Reichsführer-SS wrote to Reich Minister Speer in November 1944 that theoretically, on the eastern front alone, some 20,000 enemies per month could be "destroyed" if enough sniper rifles and telescopic sights were made available.[6]

The sniper activity on both sides grew to such an extent that they were documented almost every day in the War Diaries (KTB) of the units and bands. For example, the 4th SS Volunteer Armored Grenadier Brigade "Nederland" recorded for the week between November 28 and December 4, 1944:

28/11/44 Sniping activity by both sides in the left brigade sector, with two Confirmed kills.
11/30/44 Sniping activity by both sides in the SS Engineer Battalion 54 sector.
1/12/44 Sharpshooting activity by both sides in the entire sector.
2/12/44 Sniping activity by both sides (3 confirmed kills by us).
3/12/44 Enemy sniping activity in MA. 271-273.
4/12/44 Morning enemy sniping activity from Mazeiki and near Spuri.

Despite the intensified propaganda (for example, special results were publicized in daily orders and the press)[7], the high goals, particularly those set in combat with the Red Army, could not be attained before the surrender. The individual fighters could not equal the superiority of the Allies in her quantity or technical quality like "avid against Goliath". Yet the number of German snipers during World War II has been estimated at some 50,000 men.

---

6 Field Command Post, November 19, 1944, Personal Staff Reichsführer-SS, writing administration, Diary No.960/9, Secret. Himmler does not mention that there was no interest among the German soldiers in being snipers, and that not every soldier who took part in sniper training became a successful sniper. Besides, the losses among German snipers were very high.
7 Among others, AOK 2 reported on February 28, 1945 that the 215th Infantry Division's snipers had scored 77 kills in the month of February. The Field Command Post of the Reichsführer-SS made known on January 1, 1945 that the 547th People's Grenadier Division attained 1000 sniper kills since it was established.

Bruno Groenke was drafted on February 2, 1941 and received his telescopic-sight rifle on March 12, 1943. He was honored with, among others, the Iron Cross First Class.

Above: two snipers of the Waffen-SS. The soldier at left wears a camouflage mask in the form of a veil to disguise his face.

The same is true of the SS member in the picture at left, as can be seen above the binoculars.

Sniper Training

The training of snipers was originally based on experience from World War I, and was modified chiefly by information and observation in the Soviet Union. Though at the beginning of the war the German command did not give the training of snipers any increased importance, this changed more and more from 1942 on. The action on the eastern front showed what losses Soviet snipers caused to German troops, and as the lack of raw materials from 1944 on strongly limited the use of motorized air and land forces, the snipers were supposed to make up at least in part for this imbalance. It was in vain, as the further course of the war showed.

The basic task of the snipers was originally knocking out small or hard-to-see objects with a well-aimed single shot. This could be done either as a special assignment or in so-called "free hunting". The aspiring sniper himself was to show excellent shooting results with rifles without telescopic sights, and as for the special task, be not only active in spirit but capable and calm. Closeness to nature and cold blood were further prerequisites for success. Carefully chosen shooting teachers were to promote and develop the "hunting instinct". The designation of the victims as "kills" (like the killing of a wild animal) is rather macabre in present-day terms. Yet it was kept, since it was the official formulation in conjunction with the sniper's success.

The soldiers assigned to sniper training were selected by their company chiefs. Their participation was voluntary, based solely on the fact that the soldier had to have the desire for precise shooting within himself. Sniper training usually lasted from two to four weeks. Variations in time were mainly due to the format of the training session. This could be done in the replacement army (training and replacement troops as well as schools), and shooters were also assigned from the front, or in the troops' own training courses.

The courses were divided into theoretical teaching, in which the handling and care of telescopic-sight rifles and scopes plus the tactical use of the sniper were taught, and practice, in the form of shooting instruction with the telescopic sight or utilization of terrain. Their use in street fighting, as tree shooters, or, for example, the cooperation of a sniper with an observer or several snipers together, were taught. The training was made as realistic as possible in specially prepared terrain. Special emphasis was placed on distance estimation, since it was the most vital prerequisite for a hit.

As long as his shooting accuracy was over 50%, the soldier had reached the goal of his training. Thus every other shot meant a hit under sometimes very difficult conditions. The following principles, among others, were to be followed by the sniper from then on:

Shooting training by recruits of the replacement regiment "Hermann Göring".

Two members of the SS Panzer Grenadier regiment "Der Führer" pose with their quarry after a private hunt in 1944. The SS sniper has a civilian hunting rifle with a telescopic sight.

Soldiers who were hunters in civilian life were particularly trained as snipers. The SS command headquarters instructed all units and service offices to report holders of hunting licenses.

"When you look for the position, think also of the alternative position. Do not forget the use of the spade.

Never fire more than one or two shots from a position; otherwise you will be spotted and shot down.

Locate yourself away from your observer and work with him by signals.

Provide a clear field for shooting, and shoot only when you are sure of hitting.

At long ranges, calculate the wind and weather influences.

Practice estimating ranges.

Be quiet and fool the enemy. Nothing betrays you more than incautious movements.

Realize that you are both hunter and hunted.

Your greatest enemy is the enemy sharpshooter; fooling him is your most praiseworthy task.

Strive to gain the sniper badge by the recognized number of kills. (20 = medal without special border, 40 = bordered with silver, 60 = with gold-colored cord.

The goal set in 1944 of having two snipers per group[8] (as well as two machine-gun crews) was a failure. This would have meant having about twelve trained sharpshooters per company. In the (panzer) grenadier regiments, some 10% of the available soldiers would have been snipers! Although not without interest tactically, usually only one sniper per platoon – thus usually no more than three per company – could be attained.

As a rule, the snipers were assigned only to the troop units used as infantry, such as (armored) grenadier regiments, reconnaissance units, plus engineer and field replacement battalions. This gives an average number of forty to ninety snipers per division.

---

8 A group was supposed to consist of about twelve soldiers, a platoon of some thirty to forty-five, and a company of about 120 to 150 soldiers.

The crown of a tree as a position for a sniper had the disadvantage that it could not be vacated quickly when spotted. There was no alternative position.

Note the face mask, which was made explicitly for snipers

Scharfschützen-Ausbildungskompanie
WEHRKREISKOMMANDO I — ARYS

Bestätigung

Der _Gefreite_

Erwin ▉▉▉▉▉▉

hat am Scharfschützen-Lehrgang in der Zeit vom _4.7.44 - 8.8.44_ teilgenommen. Er hat den Lehrg. _genügend_ bestanden.

Arys (Ostpr.), den _8. Aug. 1944_

Orth

Leutnant

Certification of participation in a sniper course. The corporal, though, showed only "sufficient" achievement. There were the following classifications: very good – good – satisfactory – sufficient – insufficient.

The Sniper Rifles

The main sniper weapons used by the Germans in World War II were the 98k and 43 carbines, and sometimes also the Machine Pistol 44. These were series-production weapons with above-average precision. At the factory they were shot in at 200 meters, so that the soldiers had to derive the aiming points for other ranges themselves.

The Carbine 98k was 111 cm long (barrel length 60 cm) and weighed 3.9 kg. It had in its shaft a magazine for five bullets (7.92 x 57 mm caliber), which were pushed in from above by a loading strip. The bullet feed was done mechanically by the repeating process, which had the disadvantage of often taking the shooter's eyes off his target. But the 98k was a very precise weapon and became the standard sniper rifle of the German Wehrmacht.

The Carbine 43 was 111.5 cm long (barrel length 55 cm) and weighed 4.1 kg. It was an automatic rifle in which the bullet feed was no longer mechanical but automatic, done by a gas cylinder in the piston. The ten bullets (7.92 by 57 mm caliber) were pushed up from a magazine in the shaft and could be fired singly or in sustained fire. Thus the soldier did not need to reload and could continue to observe the target.

The Machine Pistol 44 – also called an assault rifle – was 93 cm long (barrel length 41.2 cm) and weighed 4.5 kg. It was developed to offer an equalizer to the Soviet advantage in personnel. The slightly curved rod magazine held thirty bullets (7.92 x 33 mm) and was inserted into the weapon from below. Thus the caliber diameter remained the same as those of the carbines, but the bullets were only about half as long. Thus some of the brass of the cases, necessary for was use, was saved. Despite the Targeting Scope 4, the firing performance was unsatisfactory, so that it could not replace the 98k as the sharpshooters' weapon.

The telescopic sights were attached by the weapon-masters to the rifles chosen from current production. At first civilian telescopic sights (ZF) were also used. The "Zielvier" made by the Carl Zeiss firm in Jena was given the designation ZF 39. This device, with fourfold magnification, was already used by hunters. Yet the standard telescopic sight, chosen because of its cost, was the ZF 41, which had only 1.5-fold magnification and was practically useless at twilight. To improve the situation, the ZF 4 with fourfold magnification was produced in 1943. Basically conceived for the K 43 and thus finally renamed ZF K 43, it was also used on the MP 44.

To avoid damage, the telescopic sights were to be kept in special containers made of metal or Bakelite. Only shortly before use were they to be mounted on the rifles. The containers were either worn with a shoulder strap or directly on the belt.

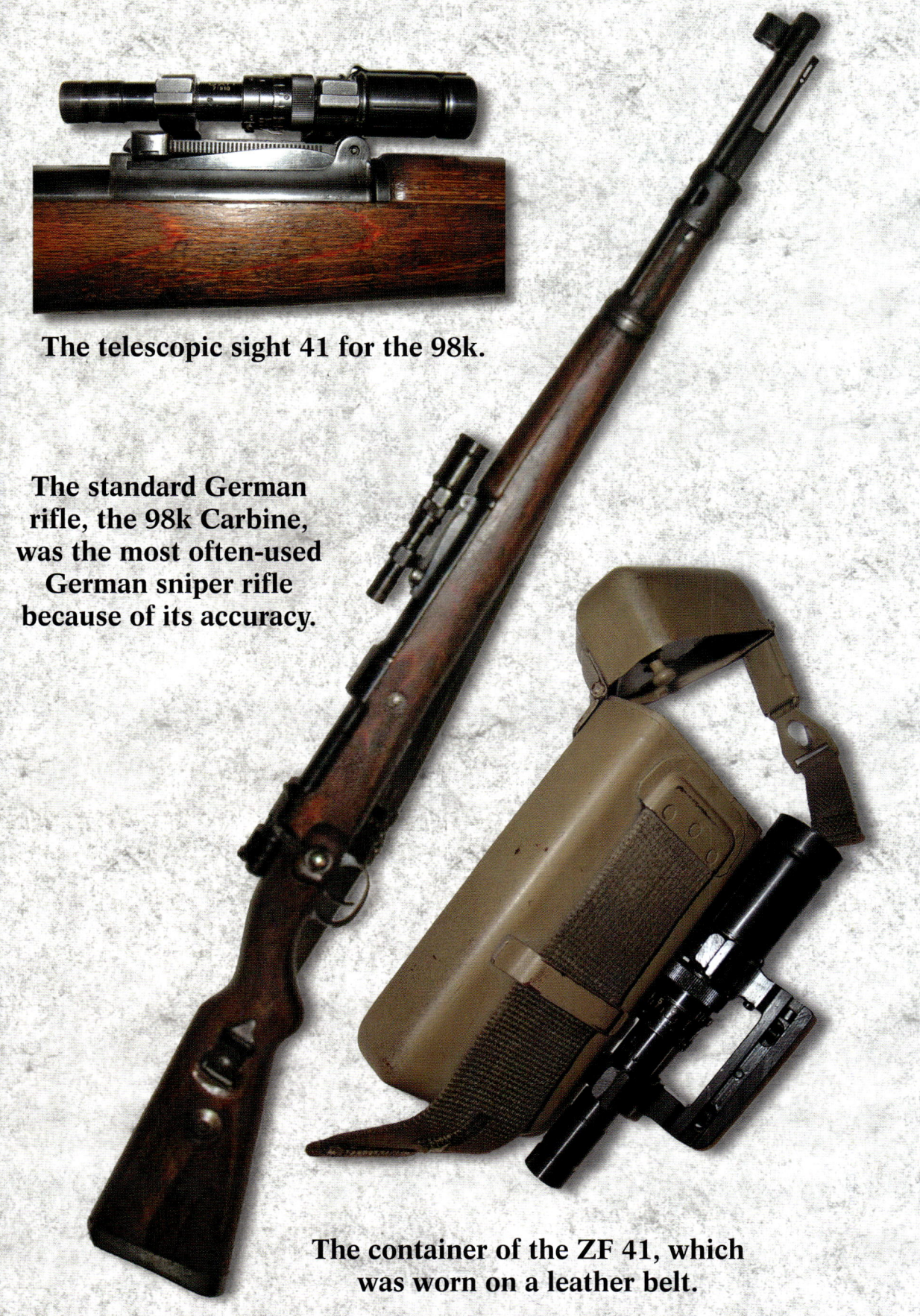

The telescopic sight 41 for the 98k.

The standard German rifle, the 98k Carbine, was the most often-used German sniper rifle because of its accuracy.

The container of the ZF 41, which was worn on a leather belt.

A group picture right after a battle. The third soldier from the left wears a container for the ZF 39.

A Waffen-SS sniper with 98 K and ZF 39.

The carrier for the ZF 39.

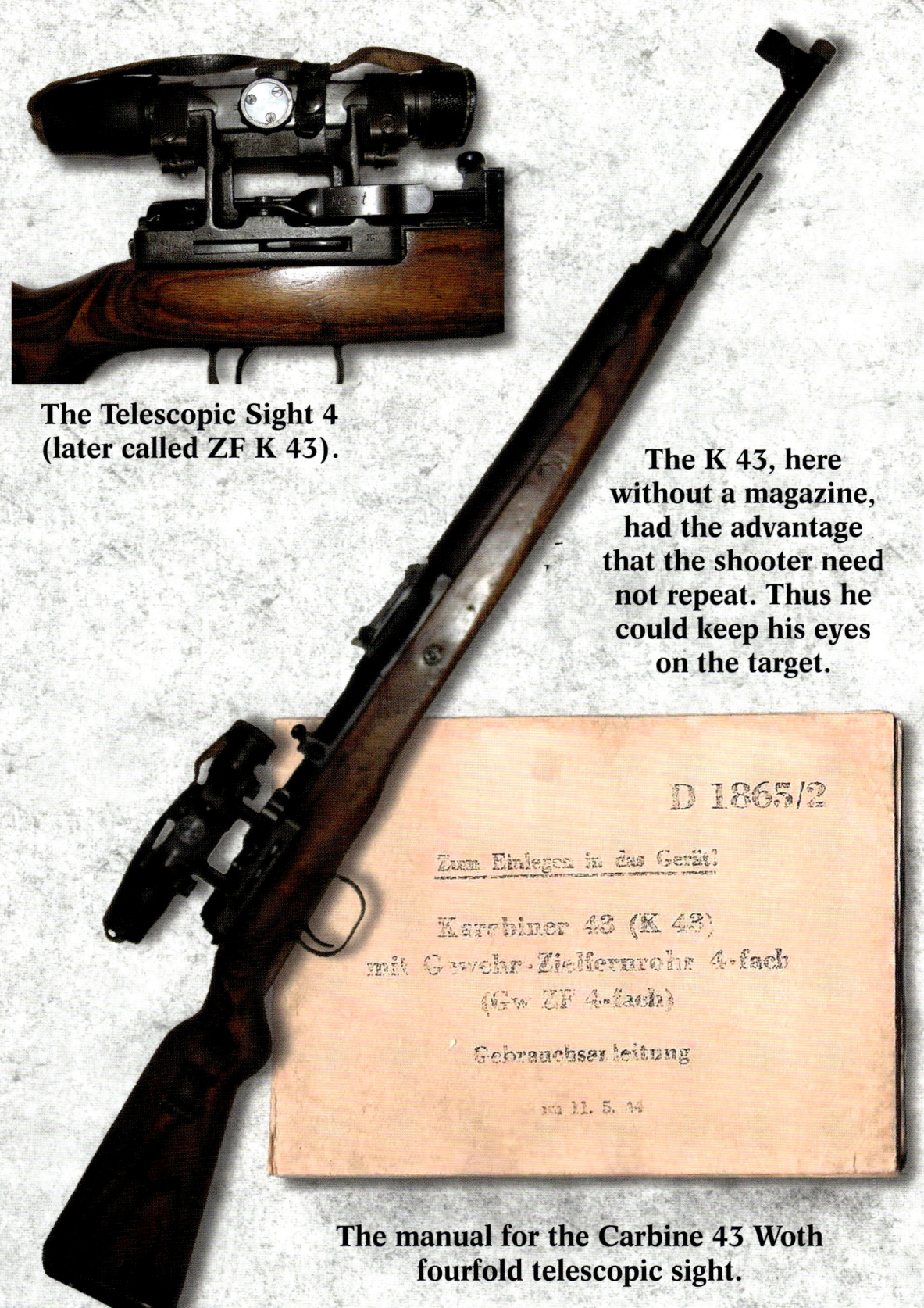

**The Telescopic Sight 4
(later called ZF K 43).**

**The K 43, here
without a magazine,
had the advantage
that the shooter need
not repeat. Thus he
could keep his eyes
on the target.**

D 1865/2

Zum Einlegen in das Gerät!

Karabiner 43 (K 43)
mit Gewehr-Zielfernrohr 4-fach
(Gw ZF 4-fach)

Gebrauchsanleitung

vom 11. 5. 44

**The manual for the Carbine 43 Woth
fourfold telescopic sight.**

The machine pistol 44 (assault rifle) already had two forerunners: the MP 42 and MP 43.

The rifle was often issued to snipers with the ZF 4 (ZF K 43). Yet its accuracy was so unsatisfactory that its use remained marginal.

Meldung vom __1. VI.__ 1944   Verband: 16.SS-Pz.Gren.Div. "RF-SS"
Unterstellungsverhältnis: Gen.Kdo.LXXV.A.K.

1. Personelle Lage am Stichtag der Meldung:

a) Personal:

	Soll	Fehl
Offiziere	520	128
Uffz. . .	3355	1429
Mannsch.	13130	2027
Hiwi . . .	(913)	(885)
Insgesamt	17005	3584

c) in der Berichtszeit eingetroffener Ersatz:

	Ersatz	Genesene
Offiziere	4	-
Uffz. und Mannsch.	548	44

b) Verluste und ~~sonstige~~ Abgänge
in der Berich~~~~ 31.V.44

d) über 1 Jahr nicht beurlaubt:

insgesamt: 532 Köpfe 4 % d. Iststärke

	12 - 18 Monate	19 - 24 Monate	über 24 Monate
Offiziere			1
Uffz. und Mannsch.			-
Insgesamt			

2. Materi~~~~

(Handwritten note overlaid on the form:)

I. Deutsche Waffen:
(In Kriegsgliederung nicht eingezeichnet.)

Karabiner	10 042
Zielfernrohrgewehre	269
Gewehre 41	422
Gew.-Gr.-Geräte	118
MP	854
Pistolen	3 568

II. Beutewaffen: /.

Erläuterungen:
†) s.Pak nicht Sfl. sondern Kzg.
††) 2cm Flak 38 nicht Sfl.sond. Kzg.

(Partially visible table underneath, Pkw section:)

										Pkw	
										gel.	O
								329	790		
								452	124		
								-	15,6		
								84	38		
								25,5	4,8		

										MG. 42	sonstige Waffen
Soll (Zahlen)	31	833	796	3800	171					959	12
einsatzbereit zahlenm.	3	118	481	1406	21	9	15	14	29	126(525)	4
in % des Solls	9,7	14,1	60,4	37	12,2	18	-	51,8	70,7	68,2	33,4
in kurzfristiger Instandsetzung (bis 3 Wochen) zahlenm.	-	17	69	246	3	3	2	-	-	-	-
in % des Solls	-	2	8,8	6,4	1,7	0,6	-	-	-	-	-

*) Zgkw. mit 1—5 t, **) Zgkw. mit 8—18 t
( ) davon MG. 42

3. Pferdefehlstellen: 14

Der Meldung wurde das von SS-FHA zugesandte SOLL zugrundegelegt.In die-
sem SOLL ist die SS-Stu.Gesch.Abt.mit den Stu.Gesch.ohne Kfz.enthalten.

The rifles with telescopic sights on hand
in a unit were tested precisely.

BESITZZEUGNIS

Dem

Obergefreiten
....
Dienstgrad

Hans Breith
....
Vor- u. Familienname

1./Gren.Rgt.473
....
Truppenteil

wurde das

Scharfschützenabzeichen

2.Stufe

verliehen.

Rgt.Gef.Std., 10.1.45
....
Ort u. Datum

....
Unterschrift

Major u.Rgts-Führer
....
Dienstgrad u.Dienststellung

A front-prepared possession certificate.
Note the fine background cloth of the emblem.

The Sniper Badge

Since the use of snipers was given a much greater importance in the course of the rapidly worsening war situation than it had held when the war began, Hitler wrote on August 20, 1944: "In recognition of the high action of the individual shooter with rifle as sniper and to recognize the thereby achieved success, the sniper badge."

This honor was given in three steps, at first only to members of the Army and the Waffen-SS. They were required to accomplish for the:

> 1st step: at least 20 attested "enemy kills,"
> 2nd step: at least 40 attested "enemy kills,"
> 3rd step: at least 60 attested "enemy kills."

Results gained iNCOe combat were not counted. The enemy had at least to be made immobile and could not have shown the intention of surrendering.

The oval to be sewn on the right forearm was about 60 mm high and 48 mm wide,[9] and was machine-embroidered. On a gray cloth backing it showed a black eagle head with ochre beak and eye and stylized white-outlined feathers. Under the eagle's head were two large and one small oak leaves and an acorn. The second step had the entire badge outlined by a silver cord some 1.5 mm wide; the third step was outlined by an equally wide golden cord.

The sniper badge was awarded by the next superior officer with the authority of at least a regimental commander, on the written nomination of the unit leader, to those soldiers who had scored "kills" as systematically trained and applied snipers. Thus any soldiers who had been equipped with a telescopic-sight rifle and used as snipers without training were fundamentally ineligible to receive the award!

Every "successful kill" had to be confirmed by a witness and was recorded by the unit in a special sniper list. Sometimes, as for the confirmation of the assault or close-combat awards, notes were given for the pay book or even complete booklets, in which the individual kills were noted, were given to snipers. These replaced the lists, from which certification of transfers or special assignments otherwise had to be filled out. There was no reckoning of earlier "kills", for only those were counted that took place on or after September 1, 1944. From then on there remained about eight months, or 240 days, before the war ended.

---

9 The measurements varied from one manufacturer to another.

First-step sniper badge for 20 confirmed "kills"

Collection of Michael Gabriel Nicolaou

In these two sniper badges, the different form of the background and the color of the yarn can be seen.

The back of the original badge shown above.

A commercial hand-embroidered copy of the first-step badge.

Second-step sniper badges for forty confirmed "kills."

Collection of Michael Gabriel Nicolaou

In these two badges the following variations can be seen: the shade and form of the background, the color of the yarn for the green frame, and the size of the black center of the eye.

A good postwar product.
A notable feature is the large acorn.

Third-step sniper badge for sixty confirmed 'kills."

Collection of Michael Gabriel Nicolaou

The most obvious difference between these two third-step badgees is the diameter of the black embroidery in the eye of the eagle's head.

The back of the third-step badge.

A commercial hand-embroidered copy of the third-step badge.

Since Dec. 14, 1944, the sniper badge could also be won by members of the Luftwaffe and navy engaged in ground combat. Here is a sniper of a Luftwaffe field division.

The sniper's position is equipped with a gun shield.

As of December 14, 1944 the sniper badge could be awarded to all soldiers of the Wehrmacht and Waffen-SS engaged in ground combat. Thus the possibilities were broadened to include members of the Luftwaffe field units and Navy rifle units.

As already noted, there were usually between one and three snipers in every company. An infantry division in 1944 usually had about thirty-two to thirty-six fighting companies, so that on the average, there were between forty and ninety snipers in action per division. In September 1944 there were over 300 divisions, so that with an average of some seventy-five snipers per unit at the time, there was a total of some 22,000 snipers. In addition, in the replacement army, there were at least twenty-five training and replacement units or schools that regularly conducted sniper training. With some forty soldiers taking part, they trained about 1000 snipers per month. There was also training at the division combat schools in the front areas. Here too, the total number of trained men must have been about 1000 per month, so that in the remaining eight months about 16,000 snipers must have been trained.

Thus in theory, some 38,000 soldiers must have been given the new emblem. Since losses among snipers were not low, presumably only about 3000 soldiers must have been granted a sniper badge. Some of them, of course, were especially "successful".

Besides the sniper badge, the soldiers could also be awarded, as follows:

For 10 confirmed "kills"   Iron Cross II. Class
Naming in division's daily orders
7 days special furlough

For 30 confirmed "kills"   Naming in corps' daily orders
14 days special furlough

For 50 confirmed "kills"   Iron Cross I. Class
Naming in army daily orders
20 days special furlough

For 100 confirmed "kills" Nomination for German Cross in Gold

In fact, the men could be so honored – but it was not automatic. For example, Corporal Hans Gruber was nominated for the German Cross in Gold on March 26, 1945, with the following justification:

"Sniper Corporal Gruber is the only sniper in the company. He has stood out through outstanding bravery, constant readiness to serve and aggressive fighting spirit. On March 23, 1945 he scored his 102nd kill."

Army passport of Andreas Wojtasiak,
who served as a sniper and sniper instructor and received,
among others, the first-step sniper badge.

Wehrdienst

oder der Luftwaffe (auch im Kriege)

von	bis	Dienststelle (Truppenteil usw.)	Stammrollen-Nr. Ranglisten-Nr.
8.9. 44	4.9. 44	Stammkompanie v. E. u. A. B. 159	
5.9. 44	44	8. / Gren.-Rgt. 952	18.1.44

---

noch IV. Aktiver

Zugehörigkeit zu Dienststellen des Heeres

von	bis	Dienststelle (Truppenteil usw.)	Stammrollen-Nr. Ranglisten-Nr.
17. 1.40	20. 4. 40	1. Kompanie Inf. Erf. Batl. 184 Deutsch-Eylau/Westpr.	658
21.4. 40	18.10. 40.	12/J.R. 163	113
20.10. 40	29.11. 40	12/J. R. 580	113
30.11. 40	1. 2. 42	8./M.G.Jnf.Regt.580	132
2. 2. 42	28.4. 43	4. Gren. Rgt. 580	494
29.4. 43	27.5. 43	Genesendenkompanie J./E.B. 193 Detmold	5737
28.5. 43	26.7. 43	Mart.⟨Gtp.⟩/Gr. E.B.193 Detmold	
26.7. 43	9. 2. 43	Gen. u. Eg. B./ 306/7	
9.2. 43	10.11. 43	5. / ⟨1.Mtg.⟩ 1 Gren. Rgt. 193 Nr. 579	
10.11. 43	23.5. 44	Gen.Kp. 5. E. B. 193 Schmidt	
24.5. 44	24.8. 44	Gen. Kp. 5. E.B. 159 Minden 17 25/44	
45.8. 44	30.8 44	Marschkp. 15. E. u. A. B. 159	

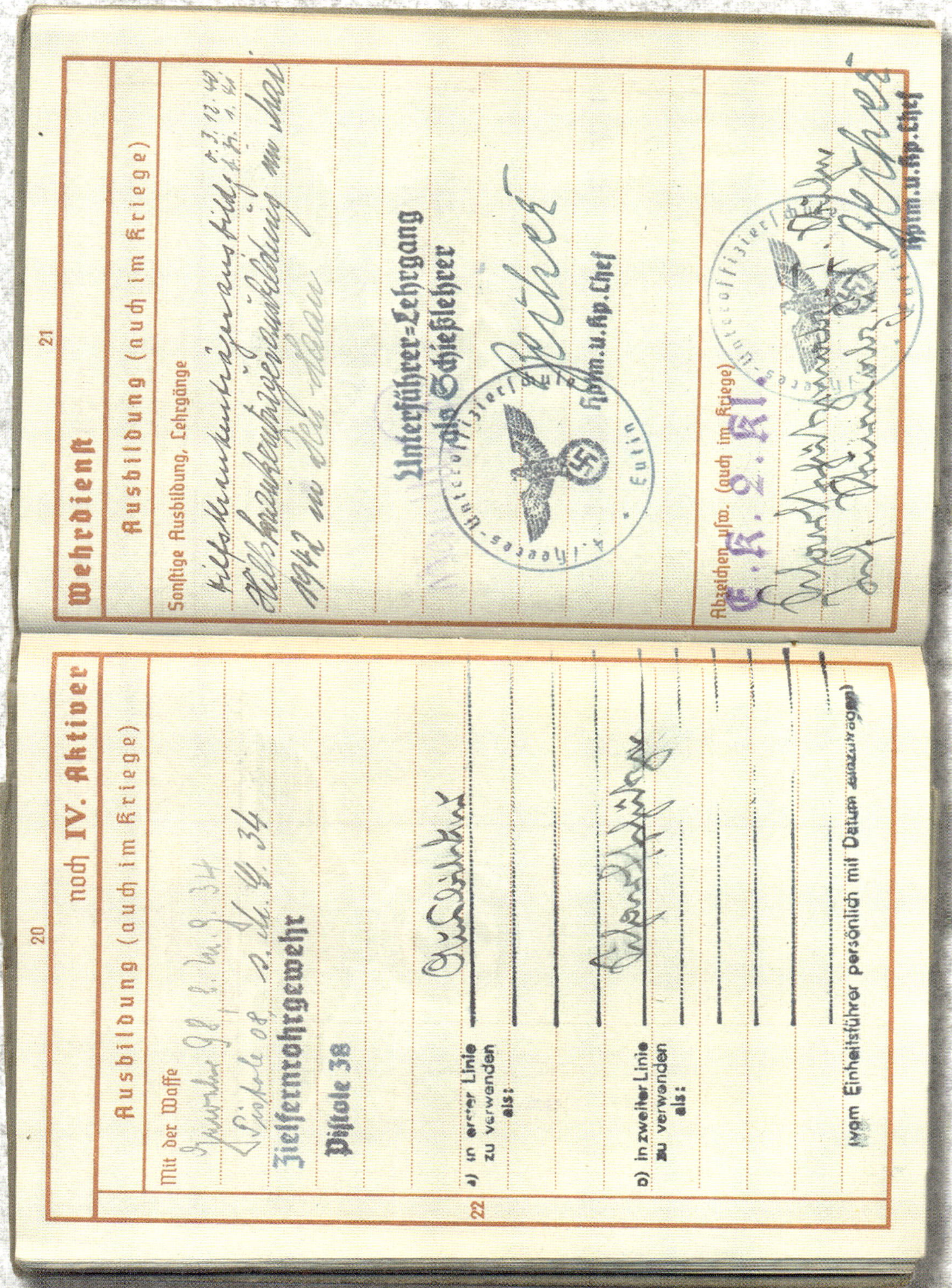
noch IV. Aktiver
20
Ausbildung (auch im Kriege)
Mit der Waffe
Zielfernrohrgewehr
Pistole 38
a) in erster Linie zu verwenden als:
b) in zweiter Linie zu verwenden als:
(vom Einheitsführer persönlich mit Datum einzutragen)
22
Wehrdienst
21
Ausbildung (auch im Kriege)
Sonstige Ausbildung, Lehrgänge
Unterführer-Lehrgang als Schießlehrer
Hptm.u.Kp.Chef
Abzeichen usw. (auch im Kriege)
Hptm.u.Kp.Chef

In the autumn of 1944, he took part in an Unterführer training course for shooting instructors. There he was also awarded the first-step sniper badge.

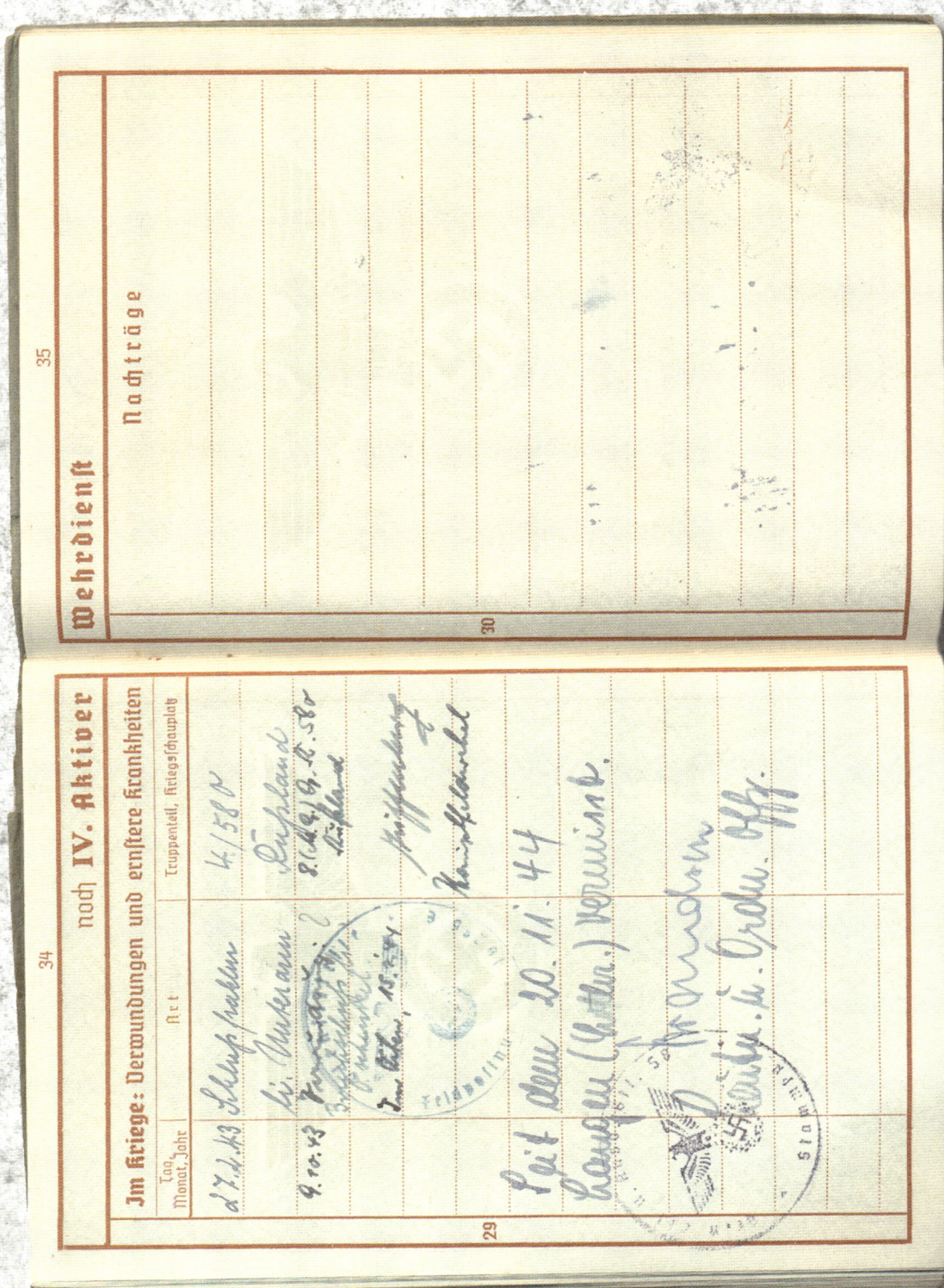

Wehrdienst

Nachträge

noch IV. Aktiver

Im Kriege: Verwundungen und ernstere Krankheiten

Tag Monat Jahr	Art	Truppenteil, Kriegsschauplatz
17.11.43	Steckschuss	4/158 Russland
9.10.43	li. Unterarm	8.14. 9.11.58 Sipland
	Inn. Klaw. 15.44	Schippenburg
Seit dem 20. 11. 44 Landau (Sütter.) vermisst.		Staskon. u. d. Ordn. Off.

**Wojtasiak has been missing in the Saarpfalz
since November 20, 1944.**

On April 28, 1945 he was awarded the German Cross. Other well-known snipers with over 100 confirmed kills, such as NCO Buehler or NCO Roschorrek, though, were not awarded this medal.

Beyond that, soldiers were also nominated to receive the Honor Roll Bar. A nomination for this medal, for which NCO Anton Schneider, who served as a sniper at the Steinau bridgehead since the end of January 1945 and the Guben bridgehead since February 17, 1945, was recommended, reads:

"In the short time since the end of January 1945 he has already scored 65 confirmed kills."

For more than 200 confirmed kills, a sniper could also be nominated for the Knight's Cross of the Iron Cross. After careful calculation, a total of forty-five nominations for the awarding of the knight's Cross to snipers were submitted. The actual awardings, though, amounted to only about 10% of them. One honoree was Corporal Matthaeus Hetzenauer, who was honored with the Knight's Cross on March 17, 1945 as a sniper. According to a press release of April 3, 1945, Hetzenauer had scored 200 confirmed kills.

While the snipers cost the enemy countless thousands of losses, their own losses were likewise high. One can assume that of the total of about 50,000 soldiers, approximately half were lost. The losses among U-boat crews were similarly high.

Scharfschützenerfolge:

DIE 547. VOLKS-GRENADIER-DIVISION
unter ihrem Kommandeur, Generalmajor MEINERS
erreichte ihren 1000. Scharfschützenabschuß

IHREN 100. SCHARFSCHÜTZENABSCHUSS ERREICHTEN:
Unteroffizier BÜHLER, 547. Volks-Grenadier-Division
Unteroffizier ROSCHORREK, 561. Volks-Grenadier-Division

IHREN 50. SCHARFSCHÜTZENABSCHUSS ERREICHTEN:
Stabsgefreiter MAYER, 6. Volks-Grenadier-Division
Obergefreiter FRANKE, 6. Volks-Grenadier-Division
Obergefreiter LUENNE, 6. Volks-Grenadier-Division
Obergefreiter WEBER, 6. Volks-Grenadier-Division
Gefreiter BACK, 6. Volks-Grenadier-Division
Obergefreiter MEYER, 45. Volks-Grenadier-Division
Gefreiter LUDWIG, 78. Volks-Grenadier-Division
Gefreiter MAIER, 78. Volks-Grenadier-Division
Obergefreiter FINGER, 337. Volks-Grenadier-Division
Gefreiter SATTLER, 547. Volks-Grenadier-Division
Feldwebel PFANDKE, 558. Volks-Grenadier-Division
Obergefreiter GSTATTER, 558. Volks-Grenadier-Division

Vorstehenden Einheiten und Kommandeuren, sowie
den Einzelkämpfern habe ich meine Anerkennung
ausgesprochen

FELD-KOMMANDOSTELLE,
den 1. Januar 1945

H. Himmler.

Heinrich Himmler awards the sniper badge to particularly successful snipers.

Sie vernichteten zwei bolschewistische Kompanien.
Reichsführer ⚡⚡ Heinrich Himmler überreichte an besonders erfolgreiche Scharfschützen das Scharfschützenabzeichen

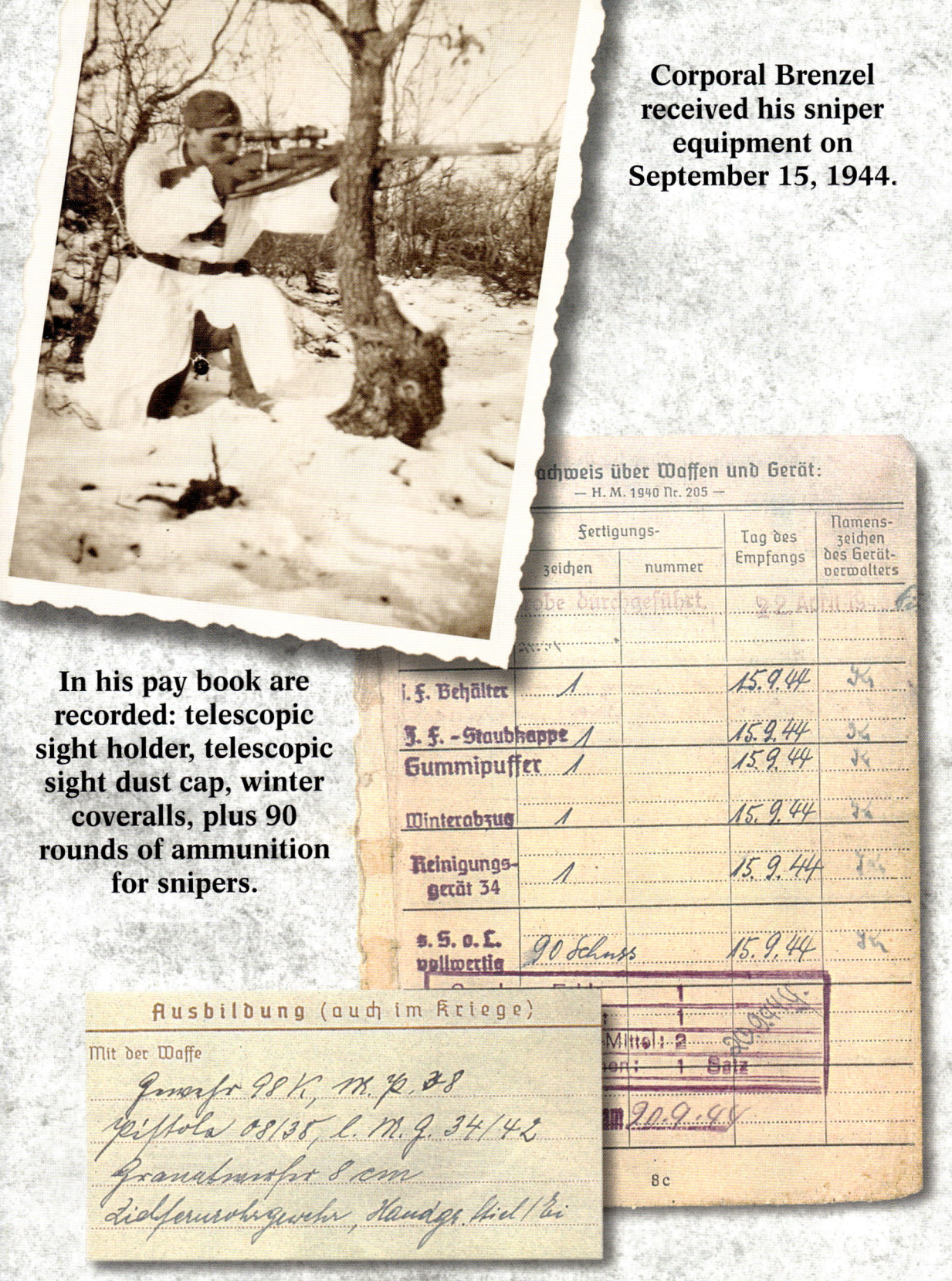

Corporal Brenzel received his sniper equipment on September 15, 1944.

In his pay book are recorded: telescopic sight holder, telescopic sight dust cap, winter coveralls, plus 90 rounds of ammunition for snipers.

Nachweis über Waffen und Gerät:
— H. M. 1940 Nr. 205 —

Fertigungs-		Tag des Empfangs	Namenszeichen des Gerätverwalters
zeichen	nummer		
robe durchgeführt		9.2 April 44	
Z.F.-Behälter	1	15.9.44	
Z.F.-Staubkappe	1	15.9.44	
Gummipuffer	1	15.9.44	
Winterabzug	1	15.9.44	
Reinigungsgerät 34	1	15.9.44	
s. S. o. L. vollwertig	90 Schuss	15.9.44	

Ausbildung (auch im Kriege)

Mit der Waffe

Gewehr 98 K, M.P. 38
Pistole 08/38, l. M.G. 34/42
Granatwerfer 8 cm
Zielfernrohrgewehr, Handgr. Stiel/Ei

8c

His training with the telescopic sight rifle was also noted in his military passport.

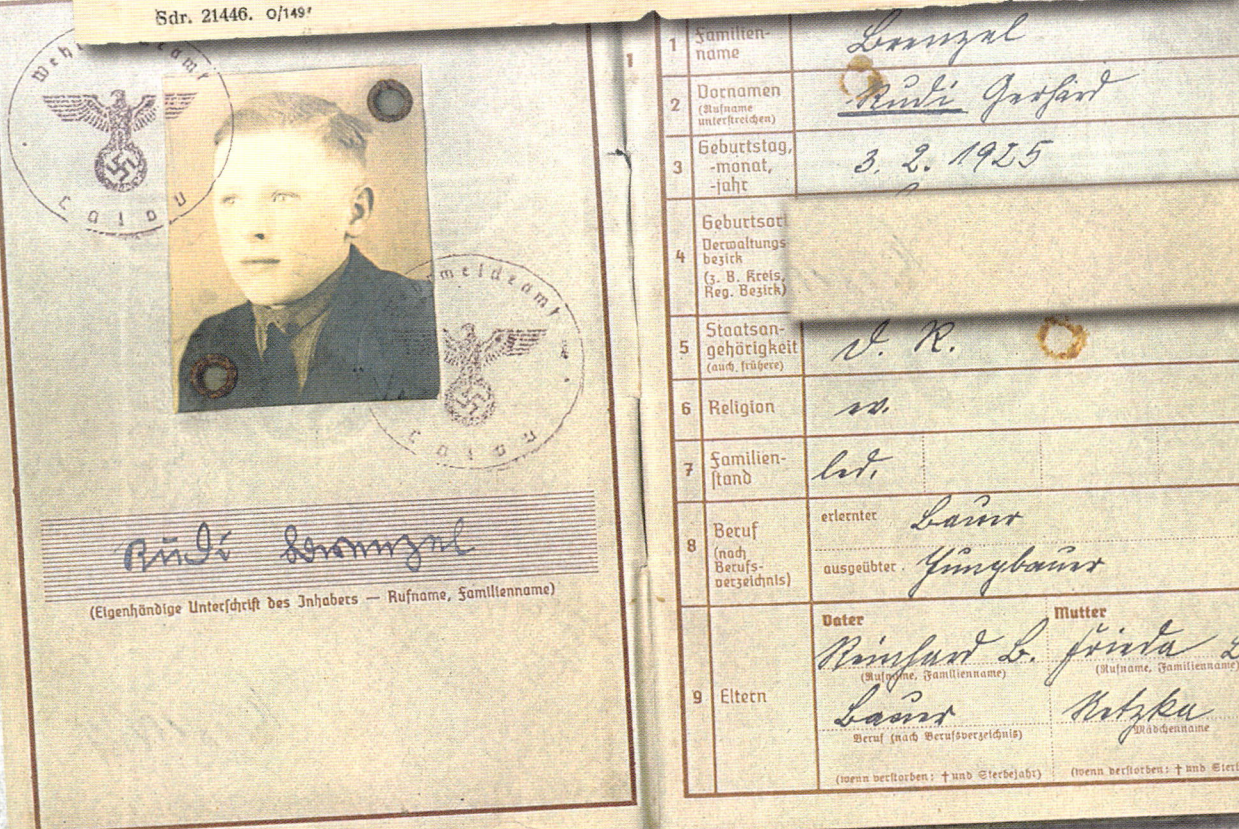

Scharfschützen-Ausbildungs-Kompanie
des Wehrkreiskommandos V

Münsingen, 16. 9. 1944.

Lehrgangs-Bescheinigung

Der **Gefr.** *Rudolf Brenzel*
(Dienstgrad)   (Vor- und Zuname)

hat am **Schießlehrgang** vom 31. 7. bis 18. 8. 1944.

hat am **Scharfschützenlehrgang** vom 21. 8. bis 16. 9. 1944.

beim Wehrkreis-Unterführer-Lehrgang V in Münsingen teilgenommen.

Eignung: a) als **Scharfschütze**   gut geeignet
                                                    geeignet
                                                    nicht geeignet

              b) als **Schießlehrer**   geeignet
                                                    nicht geeignet

Unterschrift

Oberleutn. u. Komp. Fhr.

Kurze Beurteilung: (siehe Rückseite)

Sdr. 21446. 0/149*

1	Familien-name	Brenzel
2	Vornamen (Rufname unterstreichen)	Rudi Gerhard
3	Geburtstag, -monat, -jahr	3. 2. 1925
4	Geburtsort Verwaltungs-bezirk (z. B. Kreis, Reg. Bezirk)	
5	Staatsange-hörigkeit (auch frühere)	D. R.
6	Religion	iv.
7	Familien-stand	ledi
8	Beruf (nach Berufs-verzeichnis)	erlernter Bauer / ausgeübter Jungbauer
9	Eltern	

(Eigenhändige Unterschrift des Inhabers — Rufname, Familienname)

Training certificate and military passport of Rudolf Brenzel.

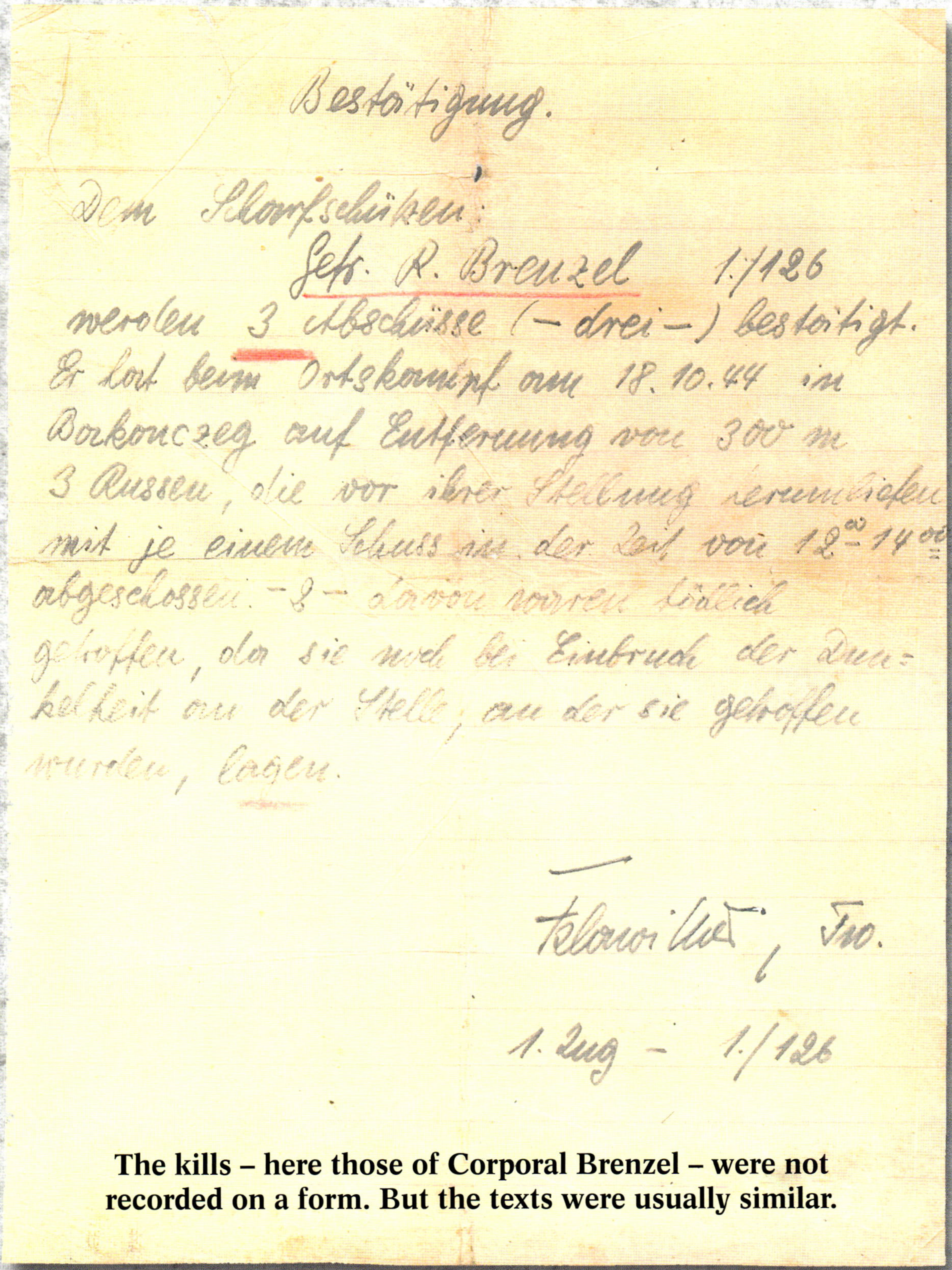

Bestätigung.

Dem Scharfschützen:

Gefr. R. Brenzel 1./126

werden 3 Abschüsse (– drei –) bestätigt.
Er hat beim Ortskampf am 18.10.44 in
Borkonczeg auf Entfernung von 300 m
3 Russen, die vor ihrer Stellung herumliefen
mit je einem Schuss in der Zeit von 12⁰⁰–14⁰⁰
abgeschossen. – 2 – davon waren tödlich
getroffen, da sie noch bei Einbruch der Dun-
kelheit an der Stelle, an der sie getroffen
wurden, lagen.

Klauwiller, Fw.

1. Zug – 1./126

**The kills – here those of Corporal Brenzel – were not
recorded on a form. But the texts were usually similar.**

Bestätigung.

Ich bestätige dem Scharfschützen
einen Abschuß am ... dem Anzeichen
...

Anerkannt:
Frank
...

Bestätigung.

Ich bestätige dem Scharfschützen
Sch. Breusel, Curt
3 (drei) Abschüsse, die er in der Stellung
südlich Pölts am 11.11.44 erzielt hat.

Klinoitter, ?

Anerkannt:
Reichel
Lt. u. stellv. Kp.-Führer.

Appendix: Experience Report

W. Rohde, then a corporal, recalled his training and action as a sniper:

"I was born in Silesia in 1924 and served in Jaeger Regiment 228 of the 101. Jäger Division since 1942. During my recruit period I already had outstanding shooting performance, so that I became Gunner 1 on a light machine gun. As such I took part in the Caucasus campaign and on the Taman peninsula.

After a shell-fragment wound in February 1944, I was sent first to various hospitals and finally, at the end of April 1944, to my replacement unit. Here, having been found capable of garrison service in the homeland (gvH), I belonged to the recovering company and saw light service. Among others, I helped the storekeeper to dress new recruits.

In the summer of 1944 a sniper training session was held, for which I volunteered. For me it was a welcome change from the boring service in the garrison. The roughly 25 participants were mostly members of the recovery company plus a few recruits who had shown especially good shooting achievement. We received a new Carbine 98k and Telescopic Sight 41.

Every day was divided between theoretical instruction, in which we were taught special features of sniping, and practice on the shooting range or the nearby troop training center. Great emphasis was placed on range estimation – otherwise one did not hit anything. It soon transpired that only half of the soldiers had the prerequisites for the course. Some shot too badly (perhaps even on purpose), the others proved to be too stupid for the theory or made themselves too obvious in the field.

My shooting performance was again very good. The concentrated aiming pleased me, and I also felt very good in the field. We were also shown an instructional film.

After two weeks the course ended and we were issued training certificates for our pay books. They stated that one had taken part in a sniper course and with what success. In my case, great success. Then I had to go to the troop doctor, who certified me as capable of war service again. Thus I was "k.v." and, with most of the others and other replacements, could go back to the front.

At the end of September 1944 we and our weapons reached the 101st Jäger Division, which was already in the Slovakian border area of the Carpathians. I reported to my chief, who was astonished that I was now to be used as a sniper. In the next night I advanced with a comrade to have him orient me as to the front situation. Nature was wonderful here in the mountains, and one could – as in the textbook – find an excellent position with suitable alternate positions and possibilities of withdrawal. I asked my comrade how far he estimated the distance to the opposite Soviet position to be, and then we went back.

Since the front was relatively quiet and no Soviet attack was to be expected, I had a free hand in the selection of my targets. So I went out before dawn to my already chosen position. It was a big bush, by which there were several boulders in the direction of the enemy. Our own positions were somewhat downhill, so I could look over them toward the enemy.

I had just made myself "comfortable" and mounted the telescopic sight on my rifle when I could already recognize two food carriers. I presume that from the perspective of my comrades in the ditch they could hardly be seen, or that they saw no reason to fire on the food carriers.

I thought it over briefly and thought that first we were supposed to shoot down every enemy, and second that I would harm the enemy by depriving the Ivans over there of their food. So I estimated the range, followed the two Red Army men and then fired. One of them collapsed, while the other ran off at once. Since he was an older and fairly fat Russian, his running resembled a limping hop. Again I quickly estimated the range and fired. He fell forward over his belly. So on my first day, in the first hour, I had already scored two "kills".

Then I quickly pulled in my rifle and my head and crept backward out of my position. But nothing else happened. No shots fell around me. But I decided not to fire from that position any more. After I had waited for a time, I crept to my chosen alternate position some 15 meters to the left of the first one.

Carefully I crept to the edge of a thick bush and looked toward the enemy with my telescope. I put down my rifle and thought, maybe someone will come to the two Ivans, I could then score another one right away. But nobody came. Then I no longer was pleased with my new position, because I myself had no protection other than the bush. We had learned that one should not move around too much, and so I just crept somewhat behind it and went on watching.

But since I had only a limited field of vision, it seemed somewhat precarious to me, and I thought it was better top get out of there. So I snaked my way backward and crawled in a wide arc to the other alternate position. I found it to be better. In all, I was now about 30 meters from my first position, but I had a full view toward the enemy. I looked and looked with my telescope, but only once could I spot a Russian helmet, which was quickly gone again. All the same, I could appreciate the position somewhat better thereby.

44

In the afternoon there was some enemy fire, whereupon I tried to find any viable targets. Unfortunately, I was not able to, since the grenade launcher was firing from too long a range and all remained quiet in the sector just opposite us.

Since for one thing it was difficult to remain concentrated over several hours, and for another, my training theories kept going through my mind, I asked myself how I could lure enemy snipers out of concealment.

Since I did not know how I was to accomplish it, I stayed in my position until it grew dark. While I was working up the courage to leave my position, gunfire cut loose all at once. Now the enemies were not to be spotted in practice, but their muzzle flash betrayed them more than in daylight.

I could spot a machine-gun position, estimated the distance and fired one shot a little to the right of the muzzle flash. I crawled immediately to my other alternate position and fired one shot a bit to the left of the muzzle flash. This too did not succeed. Whether or not I had deceived myself as to the range, it made me angry and, against my training, I fired two more shots from that position – but without having any success. I must say that this annoyed me.

When I reported to my unit later in the evening, it was clear to me that it took a lot of luck to be successful in the dark. At noon the next day I reported to the chief and told him of my kills and the obviously well-camouflaged machine gun. To my question of whether the two kills would be counted toward the sniper badge, the chief said he would have to discuss that with the company commander, since there were no witnesses. The latter turned me down.

Since I was able to make the chief understand that an observer would be advantageous to me on the basis of practical use, I was allowed to ask a comrade, who crept out to the position early the next morning. I told the chief that the comrades in the trench should do some shooting, so the camouflaged machine gun would shoot, and told my comrade that he did not need to do anything but observe through his telescope. That is what he did.

But on our side nothing happened all day. Either they wanted to save ammunition or they were afraid to get hit themselves. So I waited until darkness, and then the Russians got more nervous. Really… at some time the MG fired and I positioned my telescope exactly so that it was pointing at the muzzle flash. Then I crawled to my comrade and we went back to our command post together.

On the next day I was very excited to see whether I would observe anything through the telescope I had left behind. Back in my position, I look through the glass and, by observing precisely, could actually recognize part of the barrel. The MG was splendidly camouflaged. By merely looking, one saw nothing. I observed the position the whole day, but nobody was to be seen. That was surely because everything was concealed by tree trunks and branches. I could not attain anything from my position and began to look for another target.

While looking with my telescope I again saw the two food carriers lying there. They were still lying there when we left the position some 14 days later. At that temperature they had surely begun to rot. Even at night, when there was no more danger, they were not taken away by their comrades. They were certainly very much afraid of me.

A few days later, my group leader told me that I should take out at least one enemy sniper in our neighbor company's sector. We had suffered several losses, and one of our snipers, among others, had been lost. At first I thought it had been one I had been trained with in Germany. But that was not so. His former observer was assigned to me and informed me of the situation that evening. The main battle line had partly come under heavy artillery fire. The second position behind it had also taken a few heavy hits, and I made my way into it.

For me this task demanded the highest concentration. Since the Soviets were rarely used alone as snipers, I had to assume that in the sector being observed there were at least two, if not three, Ivans with rifles with telescopic sights at work. So I very carefully sought a position some 250 meters from the enemy's main battle line. In the trench of our second line I went with my observer to a somewhat higher position toward morning, and began, covered by bushes, to look for the enemy front.

My actual task was top knock out the enemy sniper(s). But when I saw three Ivans in their positions, I thought for a moment and then made the target known to my observer. I thought I could also fire on the snipers from another position. I fired and hit one Red Army man. The other two immediately took cover before I had reloaded.

We also disappeared from the picture at once, bent down, and ran safely 40 meters farther along the trench. Here I looked for a fairly covered position to look carefully over the edge. My observer took off his helmet, went off to the side, and raised it again and again on a stick over the edge of the trench. Some ten to fifteen minutes went by, then we heard a "ping" and the good helmet had taken a shot!

So the Russians were really on the watch here. We tried to tell from the shooting channel where they were shooting from. Some time later my observer held his helmet up over the trench again, and it did not take long before there was another "ping". Now the helmet could be thrown away! I could not locate the snipers, but we got the very devil from the chief about how we treated our equipment.

So we finished trying to provoke the enemy shooters and went over to pure observation of the enemy space. And in fact, we could spot movements on the next day. But our joy did not last long. From the corner of my eye I saw my observer suddenly fall in a heap that afternoon, and as I looked over to my left at him, I saw blood on his face. At the same moment a bullet went through my right hand, which was still holding the telescope, hotly grazed the back of my head and cut through the rear rim of my helmet. If I had not looked to my left at my comrade, it would have been the end of me!

Shocked, I let myself fall into the trench, stayed there briefly, and then crawled to my comrade. He looked at me with dead eyes … I looked at my bleeding hand, took my telescopic sight and ran back to the trench, bent over. Only then did I take my first-aid kit from my field blouse, tear it open and wrap a bandage around my hand. Some time later I reached the company command post and reported. The chief looked at me as if I were to blame for my comrade's death! A medic bandaged me again and congratulated me on the shot that would send me home: "Hearty greetings to the homeland!" My action ended again for the time being.

The hospital train took me to the reserve hospital in Beuthen. Unfortunately, the shot had damaged the middle of my hand, so that in the end, only my thumb and index finger were mobile. I could only move my other three fingers slightly. As "garrison-service-capable homeland" I was released to the replacement troop unit again in November 1944. There I became an auxiliary trainer and was to teach seventeen-year-old recruits, plus other men, about forty years old and previously rated "unusable", the basic military concepts. While the young fellows were really ambitious and wanted to earn the Iron Cross as quickly as possible, the older men could be taught by me, a twenty-year-old, only with difficulty. In March 1945 another sniper course was given, and again I was used as an auxiliary trainer. My practical experienced complemented the theoretical instruction. When the approximately 35 men were sent off to the front, I went to my company leader and also asked to be assigned. He looked at me and asked what I wanted to do at the front with my hand. I answered that I could still pull a trigger. So my name was put on the transport list and I went back to the 101. Jäger Division, which had meanwhile been compacted into a battle group and was on the March northeast of Vienna.

In the jungle-like region we were directly subordinated to the division staff at the beginning of April 1945. A captain showed us around, using a map of the camp. We were to report to various units and move forward with the provisions. Our task was simply to shoot at everything that showed itself, especially at enemy function carriers. The men were now used in pairs. This gave support when one was serving "alone" for the first time. For me that had all been different.

When I met a comrade at the command post in the morning, two snipers were already sitting there on ammunition cases and smoking. Maybe because they saw my Iron Cross, wounded and infantry assault emblems, they nodded to me amiably. A conversation developed about from where I came, my experience and success. Then one of them said to me, "You come with me and the other guy goes with my comrade."

And so we went out before dawn to a position set up behind a fallen tree that was surely 12 meters long. Camouflaged all around and upward by thick branches of the evergreen tree, and also protected from rain by a tarpaulin inside, it was not at all unpleasant.

My comrade came from Lusatia and was quiet personified. Look out, he said, the Ivans over there consist of some raw recruits. They have never heard of staying under cover. Neither of us needs to observe with a telescope. It is enough if we scan the area with the telescopic sight and then fire. He had shot a number of Red Army men in the last few days, and always from the same position! Maybe it was a prisoner unit that was being used as a construction crew and thus was given strict orders not to bother about cover and just to build positions and paths.

I posted myself about a meter to the left of my comrade, mounted the telescopic sight and put the rifle between the trunk and a big branch. While I looked at the field, my comrade already shot the first time. I looked over, he repeated, paid no attention to me, and aimed again. Maybe we were about to face a major attack, for the fellows over there worked day and night.

A little later I saw through the branches that four Russians were carrying a tree trunk on their shoulders. The range was about 350 meters. I told my comrade of the target, he aimed at the last man and I at the first. They both collapsed at once, as did the other two under the weight of the trunk. I waited a short time to see if anyone got up, but they either crawled away on all fours or had perhaps been "buried" under the tree trunk.

Two days later we snipers were given the task of covering the company's withdrawal. So we moved farther back. A year ago I had almost reached Crimea, and today? The units moved out at night, and we waited for the Russians to move in. But they didn't do that. So that afternoon we also got out of the dust. Several actions took place in the last four weeks of the war, and we made some kills. But I never received the sniper badge, although I had fulfilled the criteria. At first I lacked the witnesses, and in the last weeks we wrote back and forth. But an award application was never filled out by the unit, and so the badge was never awarded. On May 8, 1945 we finally became American prisoners of war in the Bavarian Forest, and I was released in 1947."

The Sniper's Booklet

Picture below: "shooting over the knee."

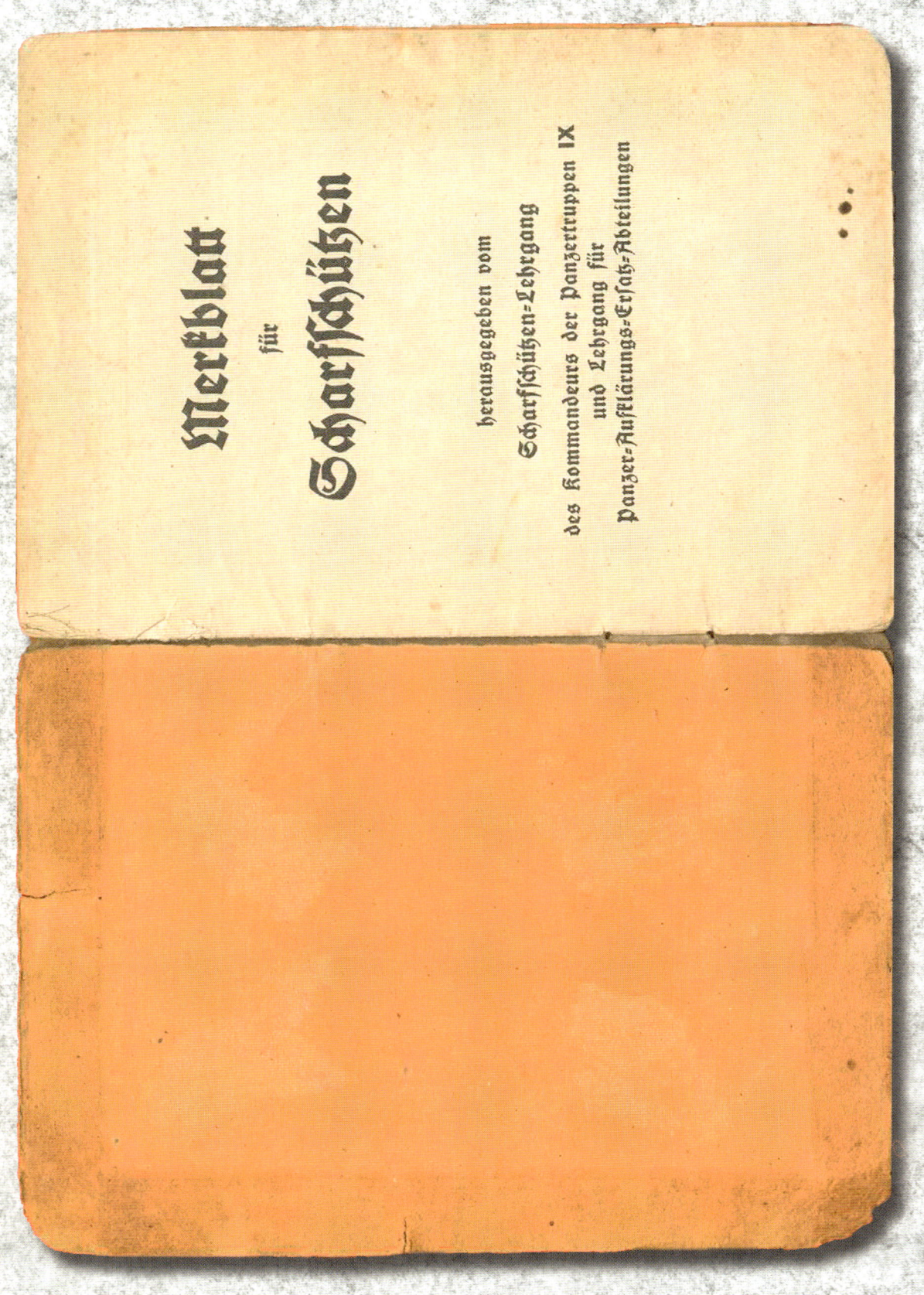

Merkblatt

für

Scharfschützen

herausgegeben vom
Scharfschützen-Lehrgang

des Kommandeurs der Panzertruppen IX
und Lehrgang für
Panzer-Aufklärungs-Ersatz-Abteilungen

Beachte folgende Grundsätze:

1. Du bist als Scharfschütze ein wertvoller Spezialist Deiner Einheit.

2. Dein Einsatz spart Blut und Munition, verhilft Deiner Truppe zum Erfolg und bringt dem Feind hohe Verluste bei.

3. Du darfst keine artfremde Verwendung finden, gegebenenfalls mußt Du Deinen Einheitsführer auf diesen Befehl hinweisen.

4. Gib Dein Zielfernrohrgewehr nie aus der Hand. Du machst Dich sonst strafbar. Deinem Zielfernrohrgewehr gehört die ganze Pflege. Hüte es vor Druck und Stoß, dadurch erhältst Du die Optik und hast Erfolg im Einsatz.

5. Von Deinen Schußleistungen hängt nicht nur Dein, sondern auch das Leben Deiner Kameraden ab.

6. Sie erwarten von Dir als Scharfschütze besondere Schußleistungen.

7. Vergiß nie vor dem Schuß die Entfernung auf der Elevationsscheibe einzustellen.

8. Du mußt Meister im Tarnen und in der Geländeausnützung sein. Dein bester Schutz ist die Tarnung. Denke dabei an das Verhalten des Wildes.

„Scharfschütze zu sein ist eine Auszeichnung"

9. Wenn Du die Stellung aussuchst, denke auch an die Wechselstellung. Vergißnicht den Gebrauch des Spatens.

10. Gib nie mehr als einen bis zwei Schuß aus einer Stellung ab, sonst wirst Du erkannt und abgeschossen.

11. Setze Dich von Deinem Beobachter ab und arbeite mit ihm auf Zeichen.

12. Sorge für freies Schußfeld und schieße nur, wenn Du die Gewißheit hast zu treffen.

13. Berechne bei weiter Entfernung den Wind und die Witterungseinflüsse.

14. Übe Dich stets im Entfernungsschätzen.

15. Erhalte Dir durch ständiges Üben auch in der Ruhe und in der Heimat Deine Schießfertigkeit.

16. Schieße ruhig und überlegt. Auf schnelle Schußfolge kommt es nicht an, sondern **nur aufs Treffen.**

17. Sei ruhig und täusche den Feind. Nichts verrät mehr als unvorsichtige Bewegungen.

18. Halte Deinen Gegner nie für dumm, schwach oder feige, dann erlebst Du keine Enttäuschung.

19. Denke daran, daß Du Jäger und Wild zugleich bist.

20. Dein größter Gegner ist der feindliche Scharfschütze, ihn zu überlisten ist Deine vornehmste Aufgabe.

21. Halte auch im Einsatz Verbindung mit Deinem Lehrgang und gib ihm Mitteilung über Deine Erfolge und Erfahrungen, damit die letzteren schnell und sicher in der Ausbildung Deiner Kameraden berücksichtigt werden können.

22. Wirst Du infolge Krankheit, Verwundung oder ähnlichem wieder zum Ersatzheer versetzt, dann gebt Dein Weg zur Front nach Wiederherstellung Deiner Einsatzfähigkeit über Deinen Scharfschützen-Lehrgang bezw. Deine Scharfschützen-Lehr-Kompanie.

23. Hier findest Du Kameraden, mit denen Du Erfahrungen austauschen und Dich wieder für den Einsatz schulen kannst.

24. Strebe danach, nach der vorgeschriebenen Zahl von anerkannten Abschüssen die Scharfschützen-Abzeichen zu erwerben. (20 = Abzeichen ohne besondere Umrandung, 40 = mit silberner, 60 = mit goldfarbiger Kordel umrandet.)

25. Merkblatt 25/4 ist für Deine Ausbildung maßgebend.

Schießübersicht für Jf.=Gewehr

Nr.	Da=tum	Art der Übung	Schuß=zahl	Ring=zahl ob. Treffer	Erfüllt
1	26.10.	150 m, Aufl. 7.u.8.0.43	5	43	ja
2	27.10.	150 g, fr. m.u.B.0.44	5	41	nein
3	30.10.	200 g, Aufl.u.u.-38	5	43	ja
4	31.10.	200 g, fr. m.u.u.6.-33	5	36	ja
5	30.10.	150 Mst.Fahn.-1 u.	6	1 Ds.	ja
6	1.11.	150 sitzt.m.u.u.-38	5	36	nein
7	2.11.	300 g, Aufl.u.u.u.u.39	5	38	ja
8	3.11.	400 g, Aufl.f.Pb.-3 u.	5	34	ja
9	6.11.	200 g, kniend.u.-3 u.	5	42	ja
10	8.11.	250 g, liegend.-2.u.0.-33	5	35	ja
11	9.11.	200 g, liegd.u.Aufg.-34.	5	54	ja
12	10.11.	400 g, Aufl.2.u.0.39	5	34	ja

Scharfschützen=Lehrgang für Panzertruppen IX

Bescheinigung

Der Gefr. Hch. Schäfer — geb. 5.7.12

der Pz. Gren. Ers. Abt. 5

hat in der Zeit vom 21.10.44 bis 11.11.44
am Scharfschützenlehrgang des Kdr. der Panzer=
truppen für Pz.=Aufkl.=Erf.=
Abteilungen teilgenommen.

Er ist zum Scharfschützen {geeignet / gut geeignet / besonders gut geeignet}
u.a. Lehrer

Sondershausen/Thür., den 10.11. 1944.

[signature]

Hauptmann und Lehrgang=Leiter.

Schießübersicht über KK-Schießen

Nr.	Datum	Art der Übung	Schuß-zahl	Ring-zahl od. Treffer	Erfüllt
1			5	33	nein
2			5	3	nein
3					
4					
5					
6					
7					
8					
9					
10					
11					
12					

Zahl der erfüllten Übungen

Schießübersicht für Jf.-Gewehr

Nr.	Datum	Art der Übung	Schuß-zahl	Ring-zahl od. Treffer	Erfüllt
13					
14					
15					
16					

Zahl der erfüllten Übungen 10

Schießübersicht über besondere Übungen
a) Gefechtschießen / b) Nachtschießen

Nr.	Datum	Art der Übung	Schuß-zahl	Ring-zahl od. Treffer	Erfüllt
1			3	14	ja
2					
3					

Zahl der erfüllten Übungen

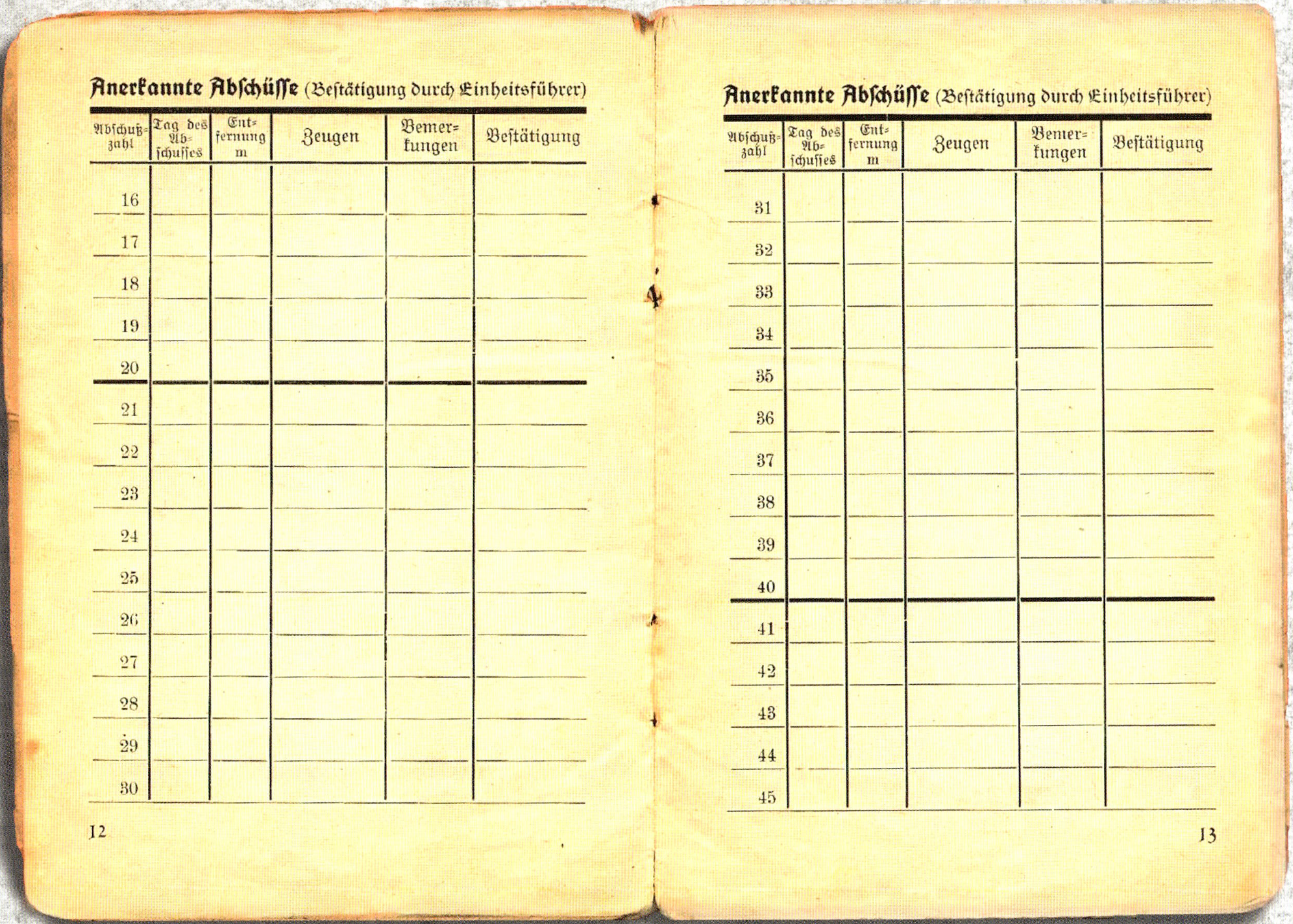

Anerkannte Abschüsse (Bestätigung durch Einheitsführer)

Abschuß-zahl	Tag des Abschusses	Entfernung m	Zeugen	Bemerkungen	Bestätigung
31					
32					
33					
34					
35					
36					
37					
38					
39					
40					
41					
42					
43					
44					
45					

13

Anerkannte Abschüsse (Bestätigung durch Einheitsführer)

Abschuß-zahl	Tag des Abschusses	Entfernung m	Zeugen	Bemerkungen	Bestätigung
16					
17					
18					
19					
20					
21					
22					
23					
24					
25					
26					
27					
28					
29					
30					

12

55

Notizen

1. Zielfernrohrgewehr Nr.:

2. Doppelfernglas Nr.:

Anerkannte Abschüsse (Bestätigung durch Einheitsführer)

Abschuß-zahl	Tag des Abschusses	Ent-fernung m	Zeugen	Bemer-kungen	Bestätigung
46					
47					
48					
49					
50					
51					
52					
53					
54					
55					
56					
57					
58					
59					
60					

This sniper uses a civilian "Hellavier" telescopic sight.

Laſſe dieſes Heft
nicht in
Feindeshand fallen!

500. 10. 44. L.0813

Bibliography

Allgemeine Heeresmitteilungen 1944, 21st Edition, p. 255, no. 255

Allgemeine Heeresmitteilungen 1944, 23rd Edition, p. 299, no. 548

Heeresverordnungsblatt 1928, no. 56, of January 27, 1928

Heeresverordnungsblatt 1936, no. 652, of June 29, 1936

Heeresverordnungsblatt 1941, Part B, no. 100, of February 14, 1941

Dienstvorschrift 1865/2 of May 11, 1944

Merkblatt 25/4 or May 15, 1943

Merkblatt 25 b/36 of April 15, 1944

Doehle, Dr. Heinrich von, Die Auszeichnungen des Grossdeutschen Reichs, Nor-
derstedt 2002.

Jocher, Bernhard, Scharfschuetzen in der Waffen-SS, no place stated, 2003.

Luedeke, Alexander, Waffentechnik im Zweiten Weltkrieg, no place or date.

Pawlas, Karl, Datenblaetter fuer Heeres-Waffen/Fahrzeuge/Geraet, Nuernberg
1976

Michaelis, Rolf, Das SS Sonderkommmando "Dirlewanger", Berlin 1998

Michaelis, Rolf, Das Sonderabzeichen fuer das Niedermaempfen von Panzerkamp-
fwagen durch Einzemkaempfer, Berlin 2010

Schlicht, Adolf, & Angolia, John, Die Deutsche Wehrmacht – Uniformierung
und
Ausruestung 1933-1945, Stuttgart 1992